History

Routes

Royal History by the Thames

Hampton Court encompasses nearly five hundred years of English history.

Begun in the sixteenth century by Cardinal Wolsey, Henry VIII's chief minister, the Palace has been extended, altered, repaired and renovated over the centuries by Henry himself and successive kings and queens.

Many great events and dramas in royal history have taken place here.

Viewed from the West Gate, Hampton Court today is still the red brick palace of Henry VIII; to the east it presents the stately Baroque façade designed by Sir Christopher Wren in the seventeenth century.

The sumptuous interiors and furnishings reflect the tastes of different monarchs; paintings from the Royal Collection of HM Queen Elizabeth II adorn the Renaissance Gallery; in the Tudor kitchens a banquet is being prepared.

Hampton Court Palace, with its beautiful gardens and extensive parkland, set by the riverside is both visually and historically interesting. A walk around will intrigue, amaze and delight.

THE HISTORY *of* THE PALACE
THE BEGINNINGS

Thomas Docwra, Grand Prior of the Order of St John of Jerusalem was held in high regard by Henry VII, who became in 1506 'Protector of the Order'. It was Docwra who leased Hampton Court to Sir Giles Daubeney.

Hampton Court Palace was once no more than a small estate office surrounded by a moat. At that time, in the twelfth century, the manor belonged to the Order of St John of Jerusalem, a knightly order dedicated to protecting the Holy Land from the Turks. The Order sold agricultural produce from the manor to raise funds for their work.

During the fifteenth century the Knights Hospitallers, as they were also called, became increasingly rich and the buildings at Hampton Court were extended. Henry VII and his wife, Elizabeth, came there in 1503, when she was pregnant with her seventh and last child.

In 1505 the Hospitallers leased Hampton Court to Giles, Lord Daubeny, who was Chamberlain to Henry VII and also his close friend. Daubeny lived there till his death in 1508. He may have built the courtyard house, which in 1514 was leased to Henry VIII's chief minister, Thomas, Cardinal Wolsey.

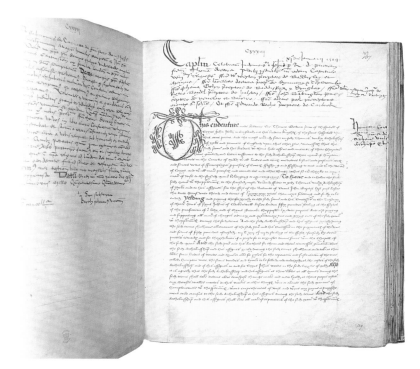

In 1514 Thomas, Cardinal Wolsey, obtained the lease of Hampton Court from the Knights Hospitallers. The exact nature of the house he acquired is uncertain, but it must have been fairly substantial to attract a man like Wolsey.

1113

The foundation of the Order of the Knights Hospitallers of St John of Jerusalem.

1503

Henry VII and his queen stay at Hampton Court.

1505

Hampton Court is leased to Giles, Lord Daubeny.

The tomb of Giles, the first Lord Daubeney in Westminster Abbey. Daubeney was one of Henry VII's closest companions and entertained the King at his new residence at Hampton Court.

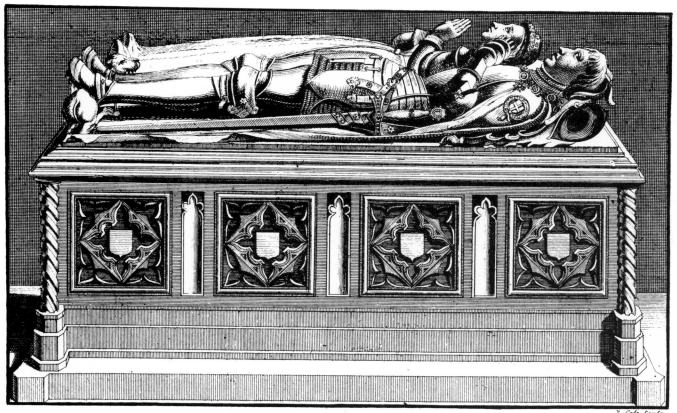

This Tomb was erected to ỹ Memory of Sᵗ Giles Dawbeney Knight, and his Lady, He was Lord Lieutenant of Calais in France, Lord Chamberlain to King Henry VII, Knight of the most Noble Order of the Garter, & Father to Henry Lord Dawbeney, the first and last Earl of Bridgewater of that Sirname, by this Lady Elizabeth, descended from the antient Family of the Arundels in Cornwall

*The Coat of Arms of Cardinal Wolsey
surmounted with a Cardinal's hat.*

Cardinal Wolsey erected most of the Tudor buildings which the visitor sees at Hampton Court Palace today. He first built Base Court, which contained forty-four lodgings for his guests on two storeys, most of them with their own garderobes, or privies. In a second court Wolsey built a three-storey range of lodgings for Henry VIII, Catherine of Aragon, and Princess Mary. The greatest honour a courtier could pay his master was to provide rooms for him. These buildings were finished by 1525 and the King came to stay. Later Wolsey added a long gallery and a magnificent chapel.

However, by 1528 Wolsey had fallen from favour. He was forced to relinquish his ownership to Henry. Within six months the King began his own building operations.

*Wolsey's Great Gatehouse as it originally appeared.
In 1771-3 it was reduced in height by two storeys and in
the 1880's it was largely refaced with new brick.*

*Thomas Wolsey painted around 1520 by an unknown artist.
Wolsey rose through the church and the household of Henry VII
to become Henry VIII's chief minister and the most powerful
subject in the kingdom.*

A nineteenth century view of Wolsey entertaining in the Great Watching Chamber by Joseph Nash. The Cardinal's entertainments at Hampton Court were legendary. John Skelton the poet could write:

> Why come ye not to Court?
> To which Court?
>   To the King's Court
>   Or to Hampton Court?
>   Nay to the King's Court.
>   The King's Court
>   Should have the excellence
>   But Hampton Court
>   Hath the pre-eminence.

1473

Thomas Wolsey is born in Ipswich, the son of a grazier and innkeeper.

1514

Wolsey is made Archbishop of York and takes up residence at Hampton Court.

1515

Pope Leo X elevates Wolsey to the College of Cardinals.

1525

Cardinal Wolsey finishes building lodgings for Henry VIII at Hampton Court.

1528

Cardinal Wolsey is forced to relinquish his ownership of Hampton Court to Henry VIII.

'My Lord rides to Westminster'. A scene from 'The Life of Wolsey' written by the Cardinal's servant, George Cavendish.

Catherine of Aragon - Henry's first wife, the marriage lasted for nearly twenty years.

Anne Boleyn - perhaps Henry's most notorious wife, executed in 1536.

Jane Seymour - Henry and Jane were betrothed at Hampton Court, where Jane died a little over a year later.

Henry VIII's Coat of Arms from his, now demolished, palace at Beaulieu in Essex.

In his youth Henry VIII, shown here in an anonymous portrait from the late 1530's was judged to be the handsomest prince in Europe.

At his death Henry VIII owned more than sixty houses, though only a few of them, including Hampton Court Palace, were capable of housing the entire Tudor court of over one thousand people. To feed this enormous number, Henry had the size of the existing kitchens quadrupled in 1529. Then, between 1532 and 1535, a magnificent new Great Hall was built to serve as a dining-room for the court.

Hampton Court Palace was not, however, famous for its kitchens. What dazzled visitors from far and wide were the king's and queen's lodgings. These buildings, tragically demolished in 1689-91, were situated on the same site as the royal apartments today. Some idea of their richness may be gained from those sections which still survive - Henry's Great Watching Chamber, the Chapel and the Wolsey Closet.

Henry VIII in procession at The Field of The Cloth of Gold outside Guisnes in 1520. Alongside the King is Cardinal Wolsey.

8

Anne of Cleves - Henry's least successful match. The couple separated almost immediately.

Catherine Howard - It was at Hampton Court that Henry was informed of the infidelity of his fifth wife.

Catherine Parr - The King's last wife outlived him.

Many of the great events of Henry VIII's reign took place at Hampton Court Palace. Here the future King Edward VI was born, in October 1537. Here Edward's mother, Jane Seymour, died thirteen days later. Here Henry, in 1541, first heard about the infidelity of Catherine Howard, while he was at Mass in the Royal Pew.

Both Edward VI and Queen Mary I stayed at Hampton Court Palace. Elizabeth I built very little here, but she did contribute the Easternmost Kitchen. This, her own private kitchen, is today the Palace teashop.

John Vardy's imaginary perspective of the Great Hall was dedicated to George II.

Edward VI, by an unknown artist painted around 1550. Here the young King, born at Hampton Court, imitates the stance of his father.

1529

Henry VIII extends the kitchens at Hampton Court.

1532-35

Henry VIII builds the Great Hall.

1536

Henry's second child by Anne Boleyn is born dead and Anne is executed later the same year.

1536

Henry VIII marries Jane Seymour.

1537

King Edward VI is born and Jane Seymour dies at Hampton Court Palace.

1546

Henry VIII leaves Hampton Court Palace for the last time shortly before his death in January 1547.

1567-70

Elizabeth I builds the Easternmost Kitchen.

James I by Paul van Somer. The King, seen here standing by the royal regalia, was a regular visitor to Hampton Court.

Charles I by Anthony van Dyck. Part of a triple view of the King sent to Bernini in Rome from which he could create a likeness. The completed bust was returned to England as a gift from the Pope to the Catholic Queen.

During the Stuart period there were few additions to the Tudor buildings, but the royal use continued. In 1604, soon after his accession, James I held the Hampton Court Conference, which reformed the Anglican Church and initiated the preparation of the Authorised Version of the Bible.

For Charles I Hampton Court Palace was both palace and jail - he spent time here, not only as King, but also as Oliver Cromwell's prisoner during the Civil War.

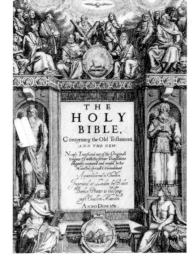

One of the most enduring monuments of the 1604 Hampton Court Conference was the initiation of the Authorised Version of the Bible.

Oliver Cromwell by Robert Walker c.1649. Cromwell put some of the contents of Hampton Court up for sale but a few items were saved for his own use. The objects sold in 1649-51 included Henry VIII's cane, staff and hawking glove, dog collars, song books, and a pair of broken organs.

Unlike many other royal palaces, Hampton Court Palace, escaped demolition under the Commonwealth. However, it did not survive intact much longer. In 1689, with the coming of William III and his wife, Mary II, the next great phase in the history of the Palace begins.

The Royal Arms of Charles I.

1604

James I presided over the Hampton Court Conference.

1619

Anne of Denmark, James I's queen, dies at Hampton Court.

1647

Charles I is brought to Hampton Court Palace as a prisoner of Cromwell's New Model Army.

1653

Oliver Cromwell comes to live at Hampton Court Palace.

1662

Charles II brings his new bride, Catherine of Braganza to Hampton Court Palace.

Charles II and his bride Catherine of Braganza arrived at Hampton Court on 30 May 1662. John Evelyn who witnessed the event thought Catherine was 'of low stature, prettily shaped, languishing and excellent eyes, her teeth wronging her mouth by sticking out little too far; for the rest, lovely enough'.

*The monogram of
William and Mary.*

*Queen Mary II by
Sir Godfrey Kneller.
While the new palace
was being built Mary
was accommodated
in Henry VIII's old
riverside watergate.*

*William III by Sir
Godfrey Kneller. William,
and his wife Mary,
intended to transform the
whole of Hampton Court
into a modern Baroque
palace. Only one
courtyard of their dream
was ever completed.*

Within months of their arrival in England, William and
Mary decided to rebuild Hampton Court Palace.
They wanted to replace the old Tudor structure with a
much more modern palace. Sir Christopher Wren was the
architect and he was given the task of sweeping away
Henry VIII's buildings and designing an entirely new
palace in the Baroque style.

In 1689, with Mary safely ensconced in temporary
accommodation in the Tudor Water Gallery, demolition
began. By 1694 the shell of the new south and east fronts
was complete. Now all that remained was to decorate
and furnish the interiors in a manner fit for the two
monarchs.

But disaster struck. Mary caught smallpox and died
in September 1694. William was devastated. All building
work ceased at Hampton Court Palace. For four years the
saws and trowels lay silent and unused.

The east façade of Wren's new courtyard in c.1700.

The Long Water, seen here in a nineteenth century engraving, was created by Charles II. Wren's new Queen's Apartments were aligned centrally on its axis.

Then, in January 1698, fate again took a hand. Whitehall Palace was destroyed by fire. Four months after that terrible accident, the rebuilding of Hampton Court Palace began anew. By 1700 the King was able to move into his new apartments.

However, William was not destined to occupy his new palace for long. In 1702, he fell from his horse in Hampton Court Park, and died later at Kensington Palace.

On William's death the great rebuilding lost its momentum. Queen Anne occupied the King's Apartments, but confined her energies to redecorating the Chapel Royal and the Queen's Drawing Room.

Sir Christopher Wren by Sir Godfrey Kneller painted in 1711. During the construction of Hampton Court Wren had use of a small office on the west side of Fountain Court. He died at his house on Hampton Court Green in 1723.

1689

William III demolishes Henry VIII's royal lodgings.

1694

Mary II dies of smallpox and building work at the Palace is suspended.

1698

Whitehall Palace is destroyed by fire and building work recommences at Hampton Court Palace.

1701

Equestrian portrait of William III painted by Kneller.

1702

William III dies after a fall from his horse.

1707

Antonio Verrio, the Neapolitan artist, dies at Hampton Court Palace.

'Close by those meads, for ever crowned with flowers,
Where Thames with pride surveys his rising towers,
There stands a structure of majestic frame
Which from the neighbouring Hampton takes its name.
Here Britain's statesmen oft the fall foredoom
Of foreign tyrants, and of nymphs at home;
Here thou, great Anna! whom three realms obey
Dost sometimes counsel take - and sometimes tea'

Alexander Pope (1688-1744)
The Rape of the Lock, Canto I

The Royal Arms of George I and George II. On the accession of George I in 1714 the royal coat of arms was changed to include the arms of Hanover.

When George I took up residence at Hampton Court, his quiet life style meant that the only building work done was the preparation of rooms in the unfinished Queen's Apartments for the Prince and Princess of Wales. The couple took up residence in 1716 and entertained lavishly there in the following years.

George II, who also stayed at Hampton Court Palace, built little apart from a suite of rooms for the Duke of Cumberland. He was the last monarch to live in the Palace and, after the death of Queen Caroline in 1737, even his visits became few and far between.

George III had no love for Hampton Court Palace. With the passage of time, more and more of the buildings were given over to Grace and Favour residences - homes for retired servants of the Crown.

George II and Caroline, as Prince and Princess of Wales and their son Frederick, later Prince of Wales, are portrayed in the coving of the ceiling of the Queen's State Bedchamber. The room was painted in 1715 by James Thornhill who was both cheaper and considered a better workman than his predecessor Verrio.

14

Hampton Court from the south east during the reign of George II.
Clipped conical yews were very much in fashion.

The East Front of Hampton Court by Thomas Rowlandson (1756-1827) The view is partially imaginary, the building on the far right never existed.

Rowlandson's watercolour of the West Front may record a rare visit by George III or his eldest son to the Palace but for the most part Hampton Court was at this time the preserve of Grace and Favour residents and a few trippers.

The East Front and Broad Walk during the reign of George II.

THE HISTORY *of* THE PALACE
1760 TO THE PRESENT DAY

The Raphael Cartoons, originally hung in the Cartoon Gallery, were lent to the Victoria and Albert Museum in 1865. In 1992 copies, painted in the Gallery in the 1690's, were lent to Hampton Court by The Ashmolean Museum, Oxford.

The copies of the Cartoons had been rolled in a basement for many years before hanging and much conservation work was undertaken in early 1992.

Although no monarch has resided here since George II, the Palace has always been fully occupied and carefully maintained. In the reign of Queen Victoria, under the care of Edward Jesse, major reconstructions were undertaken. Stained glass was put into the windows of the Great Hall and the Great Watching Chamber, and the eighteenth century sash windows were gradually replaced by new stone ones in the Tudor style. Most of the famous Hampton Court brick chimneys date from this period. Without the work of the Victorians, Hampton Court Palace today would be a very different building indeed.

In 1838 Queen Victoria opened the palace to the public and over the years vast improvements have been made for the benefit of visitors. The first public lavatories were installed in 1847. Successive Palace administrators since then have devoted their energies to preserving the Palace and providing visitors with an enjoyable and educational visit.

All the chimneys at Hampton Court today are Victorian or later copies of the original Tudor stacks.

Carved newel post in
the Horn Room
bearing the monogram
of Queen Victoria.

*Trophy Gate, built in the
reign of William III,
was altered by George II
to include his royal
arms. Visitors since
Victorian times have
used this gate as the
Palace's main approach.*

*Stained glass in the west window of The Great Hall shows Henry VIII flanked
by the arms of his six wives. The lower frames contain the arms of Henry's three
surviving children, Edward VI, Mary I and Elizabeth I.*

1835-36

William IV restores the
King's Staircase and
the Tudor Astronomical
Clock in Clock Court.

1838

Queen Victoria opens
Hampton Court to
the public.

1849

The railway line to
Hampton Court Palace
is opened.

1910

The moat is excavated
and its Tudor stone
bridge is rediscovered.

1986

Fire destroys part of the
King's Apartments.

1992

Queen Elizabeth II
reopens the
King's Apartments.

Routes
of the
Palace

The Dragon of Wales guards the Palace entrance. The King's Beasts date from this century, replacing the long-destroyed Tudor beasts which originally decorated the bridge.

The north cloister in Fountain Court.

In 1521 Wolsey paid £20 for eight roundels of Roman Emperors by Maiano.

Fountain Court takes its name from the central fountain added in 1702.

The lives and tastes of Hampton Court's royal residents are traceable through the changes they have made in the Palace and its gardens over the years.

To explain these aspects of past royal life, the Palace has been divided into six routes. Each route explores a different theme and together they show us how the Palace reached its present form.

The public and private lives of the monarchs are presented and explained, from the preparation of a banquet in Henry VIII's kitchens to the magnificence of William III's State Apartments.

The routes begin in Base Court, Clock Court and Fountain Court.

Base Court - the first court of the Tudor palace - is entered by passing under Wolsey's Great Gatehouse, originally two storeys higher.

After Base Court comes Clock Court. The great Astronomical Clock enabled Henry VIII to determine the times of high and low tide at London Bridge. On the south side of this Tudor courtyard Wren's colonnade enhances the entrance to the King's Apartments.

The Baroque Fountain Court, dating from the time of William and Mary, has twelve panels by Louis Laguerre depicting the Labours of Hercules.

All entrances to the various routes are found in one or other of these courts.

Architectural details from Fountain Court.

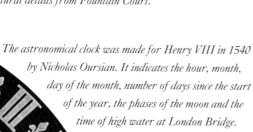

The astronomical clock was made for Henry VIII in 1540 by Nicholas Oursian. It indicates the hour, month, day of the month, number of days since the start of the year, the phases of the moon and the time of high water at London Bridge.

Anne Boleyn's Gateway was built by Wolsey but has been much altered since. The small bell tower on top dates from the eighteenth century. The clock was brought here by William IV and the doorway and windows were restored in Queen Victoria's reign.

Royal beasts survey the scene from the highest point on the Palace - the roof of the Great Hall.

The magnificent hammer-beam roof in the Great Hall is enriched in every part with mouldings, tracery or carvings such as these painted heads.

Detail from 'The Triumph of Time over Fame', one of the tapestries from the set of Triumphs based on the works of Petrarch, that Wolsey purchased in 1523 to hang in his new palace.

The he magnificent Great Hall of Henry VIII, the Great Watching Chamber and the Chapel Royal recall the splendour of the Tudor court.*

The Tudor parts of Hampton Court Palace which survive today are a mixture of buildings which belonged to Henry VIII and his chief minister, Cardinal Wolsey, who owned the Palace until 1528-9.

The route begins with the Great Hall, still hung with the priceless Flemish tapestries of the Story of Abraham which were specially commissioned by Henry in the late 1520's. Originally a great louvre in the carved hammer-beam roof allowed smoke from the fire in the middle of the room to escape.

This Hall was used mainly as a dining-room for the less important members of the court. Henry VIII himself would never have eaten here, but elsewhere in his own lodgings.

Next door is the Great Watching Chamber, so called because here the King's bodyguard watched over his safety. It is the first room of Henry's original lodgings and was only one of five such rooms decorated with great richness.

The Pages's Chamber also functioned as a waiting room for courtiers who were helped into their ceremonial robes by the pages before being presented to the King. In 1546 Queen Catherine Parr's brother and uncle waited here to be ennobled.

The Great Watching Chamber has been much altered since Henry VIII's time. Although the original ceiling survives, the fireplace, doors and cornice were replaced by Sir Christopher Wren in the early 18th century.

Main picture opposite: The Great Hall was begun by Henry VIII in January 1532 and completed in the summer of 1535. It is still the hall of Henry's time except it has lost its great louvre in the roof and in the 1920's the Tudor paint was stripped off the roof timbers.

'The Family of Henry VIII' by an unknown artist, c.1545, is set in Whitehall Palace where the painting was probably designed to hang. It shows the King seated beneath a canopy of state flanked by his third wife, Jane Seymour, and their son, the future Edward VI. On the left is Princess Mary, later Mary I, and on the right Princess Elizabeth, later Elizabeth I.

Adjoining the Great Watching Chamber are two behind the scenes rooms: the Tudor garderobe (toilet) and the Pages's Chamber, where servants attached to the Great Watching Chamber would have waited until they were needed.

A gallery, sometimes called the Haunted Gallery, where the ghost of Catherine Howard, Henry's fifth wife, was said to walk, leads us away from the Great Watching Chamber towards the Chapel.

The Chapel was begun by Cardinal Wolsey. Originally the Royal Pew was split into two parts for Henry VIII and his wives. Here members of the royal family would have watched the services below.

The Chapel's timber vaulted ceiling dates from Henry's time and is the most important and magnificent Tudor ceiling in the country. The great oak reredos (the wooden panel behind the altar) was carved by Grinling Gibbons in the reign of Queen Anne.

The visitor leaves the Chapel on the ground floor and exits into the North Cloister where Henry VIII's and Jane Seymour's coats of arms flank the Chapel door.

Main picture opposite: Visitors in the sixteenth century were struck by the richness of the Chapel and particularly by the Queen's 'closet', today the Royal Pew, which was 'quite transparent having its window of crystal'.

'The Field of Cloth of Gold' by an unknown artist, c.1545. This painting records several events that took place during the meeting of Henry VIII and Francis I of France at the Field of Cloth of Gold in France in 1520. On the left the King is seen arriving at the town of Guisnes while the right foreground is dominated by the elaborate palace specially created for the English entourage. In the centre foreground is depicted the meeting of the two monarchs and in the upper right corner there is a tournament field.

Originally intended for Queen Mary, these rooms were decorated and furnished in later reigns.

The Queen's Apartments were built for William III's wife, Mary, by Sir Christopher Wren, but because Mary died before she could occupy them, most of the decoration was done in succeeding reigns.

The Apartments are approached by a grand stair painted by William Kent in 1735. It leads to the Guard Chamber, where the Yeoman of the Guard stood. The figures on the chimney, probably designed by Sir John Vanbrugh and carved by Grinling Gibbons, depict enormous Yeoman of the Guard.

Next we enter the Queen's Presence Chamber. Originally there was a canopy over the throne. The modelled ceiling and the chimney-piece were also probably designed by Vanbrugh.

Main picture opposite: The Queen's Bedchamber is still furnished with its original bed made in 1715 for Queen Caroline.

The Queen's Bedchamber by G Cattermole from W H Pyne's 'History of the Royal Residences' 1819.

Verrio's paintings in the Queen's Drawing Room glorify Queen Anne. On the ceiling she is portrayed as Justice, attended by Neptune, Britannia, Peace and Plenty.

Detail of the Queen's Bedchamber.

The north wall of the Queen's Drawing Room shows Queen Anne's husband, Prince George, The Lord Admiral, before the fleet.

The Public Dining Room, planned as a Music or Dancing Room, is so named because George II sometimes dined there in public in the presence of the court.

The Audience Chamber gives the best idea of what these rooms were originally like. It still has the throne canopy, under which the queen would have sat during formal audiences, and many other original furnishings. On the west wall there is a seventeenth century tapestry from the series 'The Acts of the Apostles'.

The Queen's Drawing Room was decorated by Antonio Verrio in the reign of Queen Anne. The paintings celebrate British naval victories under Anne's husband, Prince George of Denmark. The Prince is shown in splendid attire on the north wall and appears again on the south wall riding a dolphin.

This room is centred on the East Front Gardens and was positioned by Wren on the alignment of Charles II's Great Canal - the Long Water. The middle window of the room commands a fine view of the gardens, one of the best surviving examples of Baroque planning in England.

Under Queen Caroline, George II's queen, receptions were held here and on such occasions the

The Queen's Gallery has a cornice by Grinling Gibbons and a beautiful marble chimney-piece carved by John Nost. The chimneypiece was originally intended for the King's Bedchamber but was moved to the Queen's Gallery in 1701.

The Queen's Audience Chamber was used for state receptions during the reign of George I by the Prince & Princess of Wales.

Audience Chamber and the Public Dining Room were used as antechambers.

The Queen's Bedchamber contains the original bed of Queen Caroline. The ceiling was decorated by Sir James Thornhill for the Prince and Princess of Wales in 1715. It depicts Apollo entering his chariot. On the deep cove of the ceiling, portraits of George I, George II, Queen Caroline and other members of the family, may be seen.

The Queen's Gallery was a private retreat for the Queen. It is hung with Brussels tapestries depicting the story of Alexander the Great. The room also houses some of William and Mary's gigantic collection of Delftware. The tall vases, made specifically for the two monarchs, held tulips and hyacinths.

At the end of the Gallery, Queen Mary's Closet interconnects with the private study of the King. The latter may be seen on the tour of the King's Apartments.

This tour ends in a small room which was originally used to accommodate the ladies of the Queen's Bedchamber, her personal servants. The visitor leaves by a back service staircase.

Designed by John Vanbrugh, the poet, playwright and architect, this chimney-piece in the Queen's Guard Chamber was carved by Grinling Gibbons.

THE ROUTES *of* THE PALACE

THE GEORGIAN ROOMS

Main picture opposite:
The Cartoon Gallery showing
'The Miraculous Draught of
Fishes' above the fireplace.

An engraving from 1720 showing the original Raphael
Cartoons in place in the Cartoon Gallery.

Detail of the basin in the
Queen's Dressing Room.

Weaver's mark from
the Solebay tapestry
'Fire Ships in Action'
in the Queen's
Bedchamber.

This collection of smaller rooms provides an insight into the lives and pastimes of the court of George II (1727-60). The Georgian tour begins at the Silver Stick Staircase, a 17th century staircase on the site of one of Henry VIII's principal stairs which was used by the Duke of Cumberland and his household to approach the Cumberland Suite.

The Cumberland Suite designed by William Kent in 1732 for George II's son, William, Duke of Cumberland, the 'Butcher of Culloden,' was built on the site of Henry VIII's Privy Chamber where he dressed and shaved. The gothic style of the ceiling is particularly interesting because it shows a conscious attempt by Kent to pay respect to the Tudor buildings. Visitors first see the Presence Chamber, beyond which is the Bedchamber with a magnificent bed alcove and then finally the Withdrawing Room.

Leaving the Cumberland Suite, the visitor passes the so called Wolsey Closet which is a rare survival of the Tudor palace. It was probably decorated by Henry VIII and altered by Wren before being restored in the 19th century. The ceiling and wall paintings are all original and demonstrate what a small private study might have been like in the palace of Henry VIII.

Connecting the Queen's Staircase with the King's Apartments is the Communication Gallery. The paintings in here are 'The Windsor Beauties' by Sir Peter Lely which depict ladies of Charles II's court. The series was painted for Anne Hyde, Duchess of York, wife of James II, in c.1662-5.

The Bedchamber in the Cumberland Suite. During George II's visits to the Palace in the 1730s, the Cumberland Suite accommodated the King's second son, William Augustus, Duke of Cumberland and his small retinue of servants and tutors.

The Communication Gallery is hung with the 'Windsor Beauties', portraits of the ladies of Charles II's court, by Sir Peter Lely. The Victorian historian, Ernest Law, remarked: '....no more congenial task could have been selected for the pencil of Lely than that of portraying on glowing canvas the sensuous contours and lovely features of the frail and seductive nymphs in the amorous court of the Merry Monarch.'

The Cartoon Gallery, the largest of the rooms built by Sir Christopher Wren for William III in 1689-1702, has recently been restored following its partial destruction by fire. It was originally hung with cartoons by Raphael, now in the Victoria & Albert Museum. The cartoons we see here are copies, probably painted in the gallery in the 1690s by Henry Cooke. They were lent from the Ashmolean Museum, Oxford in 1992. In the Georgian period, meetings of the Privy Council were held in here.

From the Cartoon Gallery, through a small ante room, visitors enter the east range of Fountain Court which contains the private rooms of Queen Caroline. These rooms were first fully occupied in 1737, during the court's last visit here, by Queen Caroline and George II. The rooms on show include the Queen's Private Drawing Room where tables are set up as if a game of quadrille was in train; the Queen's Bedchamber with its elaborate night locks, the King and Queen would have slept together in this room privately; the Queen's Dressing Room and Bathroom with a magnificent silver toilet service on display; the Queen's Private Dining Room hung with sea pieces by van de Velde, believed at the time to represent the victory over the Spanish Armada, and the Queen's Oratory with its magnificent domed ceiling.

Visitors leave the Georgian rooms at the Caithness Staircase, a particularly wide and elegant stair used by the Queen to reach both her public and private apartments from the gardens.

The Wolsey Closet provides our only glimpse of the colour and richness which marked the interior of Wolsey's palace. The pictures of The Last Supper and Scourging are Tudor but are painted over work of the previous century. The closet was, in fact, probably set up in the 1530's.

Main picture opposite: The walls and ceiling of the King's Staircase were painted by Verrio whose signature appears by the door into the Guard Chamber. Like many early visitors to the Palace, Horace Walpole was critical of the work and wrote that Verrio had painted the staircase 'as ill as if he had spoiled it out of principle'.

The arms in the King's Guard Chamber are still arranged in the decorative pattern laid out around 1700. In the eighteenth century every piece was removed, cleaned and replaced each spring.

When William III held audiences in the Presence Chamber he would sit beneath this magnificent throne canopy of crimson damask.

The public and private life of William III.

The King's Apartments were built and furnished for William III between 1689 and 1700. They replaced Henry VIII's royal lodgings. Today, after the terrible fire of 1986, they have been restored to the state in which William left them.

We enter the King's Apartments by the King's Staircase. This was painted by Antonio Verrio and represents a political allegory praising William III.

The first room is the Guard Chamber, where the Yeoman of the Guard stood. The three thousand arms were placed there by Harris, the King's gunsmith, to emphasize the military function of the room - it housed the King's Guard.

The second room was William's Presence Chamber. It still has its original throne canopy. Courtiers would bow to this, even when the throne was unoccupied. The great equestrian portrait of William was painted by Kneller in 1701. On the walls are hung tapestries ordered by Henry VIII for Whitehall Palace, but chosen by William to decorate this room. They are among the most valuable sixteenth century tapestries in the world.

The King's Presence Chamber is hung with two magnificent sixteenth century Brussels tapestries, 'The Labours of Hercules' and 'The Triumph of Bacchus'. They are all that remain of the original seven tapestries in the series 'The Triumph of the Gods', purchased by Henry VIII in the 1540's.

The Little Bedchamber is where the King usually slept, although he seems to have had a ground floor bedroom as well. All the soft furnishings in this room are modern. The original bed and the matching portiere (door) curtains are long lost.

The King's Closet, or private study, was where William III signed letters and patents and attended to state business. The door in the far corner of the room leads to Queen Mary's private closet and the rest of the Queen's Apartments.

The Eating Room, which now looks so empty, was used only when the King wished to dine in public. A door on the north side led to a serving-room and to the Cartoon Gallery.

The Privy Chamber is the most important room in the Apartments. It is aligned with the central avenue in the Privy Garden and still retains its original pier glasses, chandelier and throne canopy, all carefully restored after the fire. This was William's main audience room.

The Withdrawing Room next door was barred to most members of the court, only those named on an official list invited by the King being allowed in.

The most magnificent room, with the most restricted access, was the Great Bedchamber. It, and the two rooms beyond it, were under the control of William's Groom of the Stole, who was Earl of Portland, and after him the Earl of Romney.

During the restoration the Gibbons frieze in the Great Bedchamber was taken down for cleaning and conservation and finally re-erected in its original configuration.

34

The Great Bedchamber has a ceiling painted by Verrio and contains its original bed and chairs. Of course, William would rarely have slept here, but would have used the room for formal levees (public rising and dressing). The Little Bedchamber next door holds the bed the King would normally have used.

The last room on the first floor is William's Closet (study) with his original writing-desk. From here we pass by the King's Garderobe (toilet) and enter his private apartments downstairs.

Three closets contain much of William's picture collection and furniture, arranged as it may have been when he was in residence. Through them we reach the Orangery, used for housing orange trees in winter. In summer the trees are placed outside on the terrace.

Finally we come to the King's Private Drawing Room and his Dining Room. The latter was used for private dinner parties and contains the 'Hampton Court Beauties', paintings of the most important ladies in Queen Mary's household. The room is displayed as if William was dining using electrotype silver, copied from eighteenth century models.

The three ground floor closets formed part of William III's private apartments while he was at the Palace. The first closet, known as the East Closet, has been arranged as if William were playing backgammon with a companion.

The dining table in the King's Private Dining Room is set with electrotype silver of the sort William would have used during his residence at Hampton Court. Being served is the third course of the meal, the dessert course, with pyramids of meringues and fruit.

THE ROUTES *of* THE PALACE

THE WOLSEY ROOMS AND
THE RENAISSANCE PICTURE GALLERY

'The Adoration of the Shepherds' by Jacopo Bassano, c.1544–45. This painting was most probably acquired by Charles I but was sold at the time of the Commonwealth and is next recorded in the Royal Collection during the reign of James II. A view of the artist's hometown, Bassano del Grappa, can be seen in the background of the painting.

These early Tudor rooms, built for Cardinal Wolsey, Henry VIII's chief minister, now display important Renaissance paintings from the collection of HM the Queen.

Her Majesty Queen Elizabeth II's collection of paintings is one of the finest in the world. It is the result of five hundred years of royal collecting and contains over

seven thousand paintings. A short exhibition at the start of this route explains the history of the Royal Collection and looks at some of the works acquired by its principal benefactors.

The collection includes a number of fine portraits of the Tudor and Stuart kings and queens and two early views of Hampton Court including the magnificent bird's-eye view by Leonard Knyff, c.1703, illustrated inside the front cover of this guide. Also on display is the only painting we are sure Henry VIII hung at Hampton Court: *The Four Evangelists Stoning the Pope* by Girolamo da Treviso the Younger, which was commissioned by the King after the Reformation, for his long gallery.

'Charles I and Henrietta Maria' by Daniel Mytens, c.1630–32. It has been suggested that Charles I was displeased with Mytens's representation of Henrietta Maria in this painting as the figure of the Queen was later altered, using as a model a more flattering portrait of her by Van Dyck.

Raphael 'Self-Portrait', c.1506–7. This painting was presented to George III by the third Earl Cowper in 1781. Note the inscriptions on the artist's buttons: RAFFAELLO and VRBINVS which he uses to identify himself.

Portrait of Andrea Odoni, by Lorenzo Lotto. Odoni (1488-1545) was a wealthy Venetian merchant and connoisseur. He is painted surrounded by some of his collection and holding an Egyptian statuette.

'The Four Evangelists Stoning the Pope' is best described as a Protestant allegory and dates from when the artist, Girolamo da Treviso the Younger, was employed by Henry VIII. The four evangelists are labelled. On the ground with the Pope are two women, also labelled, personifying avarice and hypocrisy. Henry VIII originally hung this painting outside his bedchamber in his long gallery.

'Henry VII, Elizabeth of York, Henry VIII and Jane Seymour' by Remigius van Leemput, c.1667. This painting, commissioned by Charles II in 1667, is a copy of the mural painted by Hans Holbein the Younger in 1537 for Henry VIII's Privy Chamber in Whitehall Palace; the mural was destroyed in the fire at Whitehall in 1698. The inscription in the centre of the painting refers to the achievements of Henry VII and Henry VIII.

Italian and northern European Renaissance masterpieces adorn the second part of the Gallery. Among them is Lorenzo Lotto's portrait of Andrea Odoni. It was one of a group of three paintings given to Charles II by the Estates- General of Holland.

Another famous painting, also acquired by Charles II, is The Massacre of the Innocents, by Pieter Bruegel the Elder. The bloodthirsty massacre of children in a village in the Netherlands has, however, been transformed into a butchery of farm animals. Evidently the original was thought to be too horrifying.

Two rooms at the end of the Gallery remind us that, until recently, most of the Palace was given over to Grace and Favour apartments.

The Massacre of the Innocents, by Pieter Breugel the Elder. The painting dates from around 1565-7, in which period Spanish troops were in the Netherlands. The atrocities committed by the troops in the painting may be intended to equate with those committed by the troops of the Duke of Alba.

Wolsey's kitchen has remained remarkably unaltered over the centuries despite the removal of all but one truss of the original roof. The great roasting fireplace survives as does the smaller one to its left, probably designed for sauce-making and the like.

These sixteenth century royal kitchens are among the finest of their time anywhere in the world. They are laid out as if a feast is being prepared.

The Kitchens at Hampton Court occupy over fifty rooms and some three thousand square feet. In their heyday they were staffed by two hundred people providing two meals a day for the eight hundred members of Henry VIII's court who were entitled to eat here.

Today only a small portion of the whole kitchen complex is open to the public. Two courtyards may be visited. These now contain offices and apartments, but in the time of Henry VIII, they housed the Pastry House, Spicery, Confectionery and, over the gatehouse, the administrative office, which organized and financed the whole operation.

Only one of the original fifteen or so subsidiary kitchens survives. This is the Boiling House, where great joints of meat were boiled for stock and for serving at table.

Woodcut by Hans Burgkmair of 1510 showing a cook gutting a hare. In the background can be seen cauldrons boiling and a rack with ladles and scummers.

Two small rooms at the east end of the kitchens were used for dressing and garnishing food before it was finally sent up to the Great Watching Chamber.

A fifteenth century fishmonger's shop showing fish packed in seaweed and in barrels. Fish in the Hampton Court larders would have been stored in a similar way.

Fish Court, which is reached from the Boiling House, was the centre of the Tudor Kitchens. Various offices, larders, storerooms and speciality kitchens were grouped around this court.

At the end of Fish Court, the Great Kitchens are laid out as if for the Feast of St John the Baptist in 1542. In the first kitchen a boar is being roasted and a dish called Cream of Almonds is being prepared. In the following kitchens are set out pies and stuffed carp, ready to be

The Boiling House butchery today. The deer is from the Hampton Court herd and the equipment dates from the sixteenth century.

This part of Henry's kitchen was altered at an early date. In the late seventeenth century above-ground storage platforms were added and these were subsequently used as the floors for a residence which was constructed in this area. The various blocked holes in the walls are evidence of the former floor levels.

This re-creation of a Tudor Flesh Larder, shows meats of all kinds hanging ready for use above an oak storage chest.

passed through the hatches and carried to the Great Hall above. A range of charcoal stoves is being used to make pottage, a thick meaty broth.

Two dressers filled with sixteenth century implements show how the finest dishes, such as peacock pie and marzipan 'subtleties', were carefully decorated, or 'dressed', before being taken to the more important courtiers.

The last room we visit is Henry VIII's wine cellar, where some of the three hundred barrels of wine drunk each year by the court were kept. What is now the Tudor Kitchen Shop was used to store part of the six hundred thousand gallons of ale consumed annually.

Illustration of a butcher's shop from about 1499 showing meat hanging in the background and being jointed and weighed in the foreground.

A fifteenth century baker using an oven similar to those built by Henry VIII.

Today the Pond Garden is adorned with statues of cherubs and, in the yew arbour at the far end, the figure of Venus. When Henry VIII laid out the garden in the sixteenth century it was decorated with painted and gilded rails and heraldic beasts.

The Pond Gardens were first built by Henry VIII in 1536 as ornamental fishponds stocked with edible freshwater fish for the kitchens. Today they are some of the most secluded and beautiful gardens in the Palace.

Sixty acres of Tudor, Baroque and Victorian gardens are open to the public. Popular features are the Maze and the Great Vine.

The Hampton Court Gardens are a subtle mix of five hundred years of royal gardening history. The overall layout dates from Henry VIII's time, but only a small Knot Garden, planted in 1924 to show the type of garden fashionable in Elizabeth I's time, and the Pond Garden bear any real relation to the Tudor gardens.

In 1662 Charles II dug the Great Canal, the Long Water, on the East Front. This influenced the design of William and Mary's garden, with its three great avenues of yew trees.

The Privy Garden on the south was originally William III's private garden, laid out with tightly clipped hollies and yews. By 1991 the garden was extremely overgrown and a decision was taken to restore it to its original 1702 layout. The Privy Garden is one of the best documented gardens in England and a wealth of historical records survived which, together with painstaking archaeology, enabled the restoration to be undertaken. A particularly fine view of the restored garden can be enjoyed from the King's State Apartments.

The East Front of the Palace seen from the Great Fountain Garden.

The statue of The Three Graces, dating from the early nineteenth century, was cast in Paris and originally designed as a fountain.

The Maze was planted in the 1690s by William's gardeners as part of a formal layout called the Wilderness. It is the only part remaining of the original.

Planted in 1768, the Great Vine still produces an annual crop of delicious grapes.

The Mantegna Gallery was originally an orangery built to house Mary II's botanical specimens. Today it holds Andrea Mantegna's 'Triumphs of Caesar', nine of the most valuable and important paintings in the Queen's collection. They were acquired by Charles I in 1629 and have hung at Hampton Court Palace ever since.

William III built the Banqueting House in 1700 on the foundations of a Tudor building. It was designed for intimate riverside parties. The lavish decorations are by Verrio.

46

The tiltyard on the north of the Palace was built by Henry VIII for tournaments. It was divided up into smaller gardens in the eighteenth and nineteenth centuries and it now contains the Palace restaurant, built next to one of Henry VIII's tiltyard towers.

During the reign of William III this entire area, known as the Wilderness, was planted out with tall clipped evergreens in geometric patterns.

The Great Vine was attracting attention as early as 1800 and during the nineteenth century could produce over two thousand lbs of grapes in a good year.

One of Jerome K Jerome's Three Men in a Boat declared the maze 'very simple...it's absurd to call it a maze', only to become completely lost.

Great Fountain Garden.

Other Historic Royal Palaces to visit

THE TOWER OF LONDON
Britain's foremost historical attraction

Work on the Tower was begun by William the Conqueror in the eleventh century. Since then it has been a fortress, prison, arsenal, treasury and palace. With the Crown Jewels, the Yeoman Warders and the Royal Armouries, it remains Britain's most absorbing historical landmark.

Enquiries telephone 0171 709 0765

THE BANQUETING HOUSE
WHITEHALL PALACE
The original setting for royal banquets

This one building is now the only remaining part of Whitehall Palace. It dates from 1619 and was designed by the renowned architect Inigo Jones. Charles I, the only English monarch to be executed, met his fate here.

Enquiries telephone 0171 839 8918

KENSINGTON PALACE
The 'undiscovered' Royal Palace

Birthplace of Queen Victoria, the Palace was first acquired by William III and Mary II in 1689. It is still lived in by the Royal Family today. The public have access to the State Apartments and the fascinating Royal Ceremonial Dress Collection.

Enquiries telephone 0171 937 9561

KEW PALACE
The Royal Home in the Gardens

Dating from 1631, this is one of the smaller Royal Palaces and is set in the Royal Botanic Gardens. It provides an intriguing glimpse of royal domestic life in the early part of the nineteenth century.

Enquiries telephone 0181 940 3321

QUEEN CHARLOTTE'S COTTAGE
The Royal Summer House in the Gardens

The Cottage, also in the Royal Botanic Gardens at Kew, was built in 1772 and named after Queen Charlotte, consort to George III. The royal family used it as a summer house and often took tea there.

Enquiries telephone 0181 940 3321

PHOTOGRAPHS REPRODUCED BY KIND PERMISSION OF THE FOLLOWING:

Historic Royal Palaces (Crown Copyright): pages 6, 9, 13, 15, 28; The Royal Collection © 1993 Her Majesty The Queen: inside front cover, pages 8, 9, 10, 12, 13, 20, 23, 25, 36, 37, 38, 39; The British Library: pages 5, 10, 42–3; The National Portrait Gallery, London: pages 6, 8, 10, 13; The Board of Trustees of the Victoria and Albert Museum: pages 7, 15; The Trustees of the British Museum: pages 5, 10–11; Kunsthistorisches Museum, Vienna: page 8; The Society of Antiquaries of London: page 11; The Warburg Institute: page 41; Stadtbibliothek Nurnberg: page 43; His Grace the Archbishop of Canterbury: page 9; Service Photographique des Archives Nationales, Paris: page 6; The Bodleian Library, Oxford (MS. Douce 363): page 7; The Louvre Museum, Paris: page 9; The property of the late Col. J.L. Adams, J.P., T.D., D.L., of Holyland, Pembroke: page 11; The College of Arms, London (Bath Book p.11): page 14; Les Strudwick: page 17; Anthony Burrett: page 35; The Museum of the Order of St. John: page 4

HAMPTON COURT PALACE WOULD ALSO LIKE TO ACKNOWLEDGE THE FOLLOWING CONTRIBUTIONS:
Written by Simon Thurley; picture research by Clare Murphy; principal photography by Earl Beesley; Designed by Event Communications Ltd

Printed by The Woodway Group PLC